Who Belongs Here?

Teacher's Guide

Who Belongs Here?

Teacher's Guide

Margy Burns Knight
Thomas V. Chan

with details from the original *Who Belongs Here?* illustrations
by Anne Sibley O'Brien

Tilbury House, Publishers
Gardiner, Maine

Tilbury House, Publishers
2 Mechanic Street
Gardiner, Maine 04345

10 9 8 7 6 5 4

Contents

Acknowledgements

Special thanks to Winnie McPhederan, Dianne Webb, Linda Ward Burgess, Ruth Dader, Project Synergy (Kennebunk, Maine), Sandy Nevins, Mara Burns, Gail Garthwait, Paul Hazelton, Steve Raph, Winthrop (Maine) Elementary School staff, Karen Richards Toothaker, Nancy McGinnis, Justine Denison, Lois Beddy, Wendy Heindlmeyer, Terri Durgan, Nancy Kelly, Barbara Livingston, and Kathryn Markovchick.

—Margy Burns Knight

To the students, parents, and staffs of both Florence Nightingale School and River Elm School who believe in me, I fondly dedicate this book and its beautiful message.

—Thomas V. Chan

Introduction

Tom Chan and I wrote this activity guide to continue the dialogue begun in *Who Belongs Here? An American Story*. This picturebook, published in 1993 by Tilbury House, Publishers, was written by me and illustrated by Anne Sibley O'Brien.

The guide follows the text and focuses on developing listening, thinking, and writing skills. Many of the activities stress the crucial connection between classroom and community and can be adapted to your teaching style and your students' learning styles.

It is important to give your students time to discuss issues raised in the book — immigration, name-calling, prejudice, heritage, language, and traditions, to name a few. As a teacher, you can help your students find further information by reading, writing, and asking questions.

Writer David Mura asks, "How do we teach children about history in a way that does not sugarcoat the past, that does not deny the complexities of our heritage as Americans?" By encouraging dialogue and fostering a safe environment in which each student's voice can be heard, you will be able to use *Who Belongs Here?* to teach children honestly about their history, their lives now, and their future.

—Margy Burns Knight

Who Belongs Here?

Teacher's Guide

1. Looking at Illustrations — What Do You See?

a) Looking at the illustrations in *Who Belongs Here?* can be a good way to generate questions, discussion, and dialogue. Sample questions include:

> What do you see?
> What is this picture about?
> Does it have anything to do with you?
> Does it look like any other picture?
> What else would you like to know about this picture?
> Is there anyone in our community who could tell us more about this picture?

b) Expand on these questions by referring to the question matrix below. This format can be used as a warm-up exercise for many of the activities in the guide. Your students will need some information before embarking on many of these activities. For example, students must be familiar with Cambodian history before they can understand Cambodian refugees.

c) Answer these questions in small groups or with the entire class before reading the book. You could use a few or all of the illustrations. Chart students' responses on a large piece of paper and add to the chart after the book is read and as activities are completed. Use your students' responses to begin writing, vocabulary, spelling, or research projects. Encourage your students to think on their own and come up with their own questions.

	EVENT	SITUATION	CHOICE	PERSON	REASON	MEANS
PRESENT	1. What Is?	2. Where/When Is?	3. Which Is?	4. Who Is?	5. Why Is?	6. How Is?
PAST	7. What Did?	8. Where/When Did?	9. Which Did?	10. Who Did?	11. Why Did?	12. How Did?
POSSIBILITY	13. What Can?	14. Where/When Can?	15. Which Can?	16. Who Can?	17. Why Can?	18. How Can?
PROBABILITY	19. What Would?	20. Where/When Will?	21. Which Would?	22. Who Would?	23. Why Would?	24. How Would?
PREDICTION	25. What Will?	26. Where/When Will?	27. Which Will?	28. Who Will?	29. Why Will?	30. How Will?
IMAGINATION	31. What Might?	32. Where/When Might?	33. Which Might?	34. Who Might?	35. Why Might?	36. How Might?

2. Who Is on the Cover?

a) Illustrator Annie O'Brien photographed sixteen children at an elementary school in Portland, Maine, to use as models for the cover of *Who Belongs Here?* Two of the children are my friends; the boy in the green shirt is a composite. Ask your students how they think illustrators decide what or who to show on a book's cover. What other book covers show only children? Ask students to go to the library and check out some of these books. How are the covers the same? How are they different?

b) Students may want to make their own book covers using classmates as models.

c) They may want to make a new cover for *Who Belongs Here?* without children, using just colors, symbols, or objects.

d) Invite an illustrator to your classroom.

3. Create a Storymap and Write About It

a) The illustration that looks like a child's drawing (at the beginning of *Who Belongs Here?*) was re-created from my sixth grade Cambodian students' artwork. They were asked to report on a country of their choice. Many chose Thailand but had difficulty understanding the material in reference books. I asked them what country they knew best and how they could teach me about it. They said Cambodia and asked if they could draw pictures. From the pictures they wrote stories and produced two videos, *The Cambodia I Remember* and *America My New Country*, with their voices telling the stories.

My students felt strongly that their stories should include descriptions of life in Cambodia before the war. Many told stories that they had heard from family members. They drew sunsets and flowers and talked endlessly about their food, games, friends, families, and celebrations.

b) It is important that your students learn about Cambodia. The question matrix on page 1 is a useful way to gather information.

c) We call Nary's picture of his life in Cambodia a storymap. When your students finish talking about Nary's storymap, they could create their own storymaps. They needn't portray their entire lives; students may want to create storymaps about a special journey or a special meal. Allow time, space, lots of colors, and different sizes of paper. Some students may want to cut pictures out of magazines, while others may want to use family photos. Share your storymap with your students, so they can see that you have a story, too!

d) You may want to brainstorm with the class about some of the elements they might include in a storymap and leave the list in a visible spot, so students can refer to it as they work.

e) When the students are done, they may want to compare their maps with Nary's, looking especially for similarities. For example, Nary eats, plays soccer, has a family, goes to school, and has memories and dreams.

f) Students could use their storymaps to write stories. Final, revised copies could be typed and displayed with the storymaps. In preparing *Who Belongs Here?* for publication, Annie O'Brien and I created text-and-picture combinations called storyboards. Our storyboards underwent at least thirty revisions before the book went to press.

4. Cambodian Folktales

a) Obtain a copy of Cambodian folktales for children and read one or two to your class.

b) Ask each child to create his / her own folktale using characters similar to those they read about in the Cambodian tales.

c) Share folktales from other lands with your students.

5. What Is Your Name?

a) I chose the name Nary for my story because Nary was one of my first Cambodian students. My parents named me Margaret Mary Burns. I was named Margaret after my Great-aunt Peg, but I have always been called Margy, with a hard G. My dad thinks the spelling of Burns used to be Byrnes and was changed from the Irish to the Scottish spelling after his grandparents arrived in Philadelphia.

b) Ask your students why they have their names. (They may have to ask someone in their family.) I met a woman who was named after a nurse in the hospital where she was born and a boy who is a seventh-generation Cole.

c) Using multicolored paper, have each student trace his / her foot with shoes on. Ask students to write a short story about their name and copy the final draft on their foot. (I use feet because Nary's story is a journey and he began his journey to the United States on foot. You could use hands, or students could cut out the shape of their first initial.) Some students may want to use both feet and tell stories about their first and middle or first and last names.

d) Find a spot in your classroom or school to display the feet in a pattern of your students' choice. In one school, students displayed their story-feet in a library stairwell.

e) Ask other teachers, staff, and community members to tell stories about their names. You may want to display the stories in the community library or a bank or community center.

6. Flags

a) Ask your students why countries and states have flags.

b) Have students describe several familiar flags.

c) Ten countries are mentioned in *Who Belongs Here?*: Cambodia, Thailand, United States, Canada, Italy, Haiti, Ireland, Vietnam, China, and Poland. In groups, students could research the national flag of each country, tell how it was designed, and show any changes that have been made in the design. Drawings of these flags could be displayed in your classroom or hallway. Younger students may want to have a flag parade.

d) Students could make personal flags, portraying whatever is most important to them.

e) Classroom or school flags could also be designed and displayed.

f) For a community flag project, students could find out what flags are displayed in their community. They may want to invite community members to talk about some of these flags.

7. What Would You Take if You Were a Refugee?

As an English-as-a-Second-Language teacher, I worked closely with Barbara Livingston, a middle school social studies teacher. When my students asked what could be done to help other kids understand what it is like to be a refugee, this is what Barbara and I did:

a) First, we engaged students in a discussion about refugees using the question matrix. (You might also show the beginning of the Disney film *The Girl Who Spelled Freedom*, available at most video stores, to give students a sense of a refugee's escape.)

b) Next, we asked groups (including some refugee students and adults we had recruited) to think about what they would take with them if forced to leave their country as refugees. One Cambodian girl said, "Oh, you can't take your dog, the soldiers will hear it bark and kill you."

c) Students then numbered their papers vertically, one to ten, and listed ten things they would take with them if they had to flee. (We required that each student work alone.) Below are some of the items students listed:

1. books
2. food
3. gun
4. hairdryer
5. matches
6. photographs
7. dog
8. blanket
9. tent
10. cookstove

d) You can use this list to show your students how to prioritize. Don't show them the list until they have had time to compile their own lists. Then tell them that they can carry only two things. What would they choose?

Start by asking questions about items on the sample list. Which would you take, books or food? If food is the answer, number two gets a point. If books is the answer, number one gets the point. Continue asking questions about numbers one and three, one and four, one and five, until number one has been compared to all the items. Then begin with number two and compare it to all the other items. Each time a choice is made, a point is given. After number nine is compared with ten, add up the points. The top two items are the items you take with you.

e) This exercise challenges students to think about what material objects are most important to them. When each student has his / her top two items, you may ask them to talk about them, write them on the board, or hand them in without their names. Later you could display the responses and talk about them together. The responses could be used as a springboard for sentence, paragraph, or essay writing.

f) Invite to your classroom people from your community who have left their country. Ask them what they brought with them and why. Nary's family brought very little. What did other Cambodians bring? Your visitor doesn't have to be a refugee. Many people have chosen to come to the United States as immigrants. Continue your discussions with the following books.

Reading Connections

1. Ashabranner, Brent, *Still a Nation of Immigrants, The New Americans Into a Strange Land*, Cobblehill, New York, 1993. "Who are today's immigrants? Why do they come to America?" These and other questions are asked and answered in this nonfiction book.

2. Bresnick-Perry, Roslyn, *Leaving for America*, Children's Book Press, Emeryville, California, 1993. A young Jewish Russian girl moves to the United States.

3. Bunting, Eve, *How Many Days to America?*, Clarion Books, New York, 1988. A family's seagoing attempt to flee a repressive Caribbean country for America.

4. Chandler, David P., *A History of Cambodia*, Westview Press, Boulder, Colorado, 1983.

5. Chandler, David P., *Favourite Stories From Cambodia*, Heinemann Asia, Hong Kong, 1978.

6. Chandler, David P., *The Land and People of Cambodia*, Harper Collins, New York, 1991.

7. Crew, Linda, *Children of the River*, Dell, New York, 1989. Explores the feelings of 17-year-old Sundara who fled the Khmer Rouge to live in Oregon.

8. Dawson, M., *Over Here It's Different*, Macmillan, New York, 1993. A seven-year-old moves from the Dominican Republic to New York.

9. Freedman, Russell, *Immigrant Kids*, Dutton, New York, 1980. Photographs of immigrant children at school and at work.

10. Goldfarb, M., *Fighters, Refugees, Immigrants*, Carolrhoda Books, Minneapolis, 1982. Photo-essay of a volunteer doctor's experience with the Hmong people.

11. Gordon, Ginger, *My Two Worlds*, Clarion, New York, 1993. A young girl in New York returns to the Dominican Republic for Christmas.

12. Graff, Nancy Price, *Where the River Runs, A Portrait of a Refugee Family*, Little, Brown, Boston, 1993. The life of a Cambodian family in Boston.

13. Ho, Minfong, *The Clay Marble*, Farrar, Strauss and Giroux, New York, 1991. Factual, honest book about war-torn Cambodia.

14. Howlett, Bud, *I'm New Here*, Houghton Mifflin, Boston, 1993. Story of a fifth grader who has moved from El Salvador to the United States.

15. Huynh, Quang Nhuong, *The Land I Lost: Adventures of a Boy in Vietnam*, Harper, New York, 1990. Fifteen true stories of the author's childhood.

16. Kidd, Diana, *Onion Tears*, Beech Tree, New York, 1989. Vietnamese-born Nam-Huong wants to adjust to her new life in Australia.

17. Lasky, Kathyrn, *The Night Journey*, Warne, New York, 1981. Nana tells of her escape from Russia.

18. Palacco, Patricia, *The Keeping Quilt*, Simon and Schuster, New York, 1988. A picturebook about four generations of an immigrant Jewish family.

19. Paulsen, Gary, *The Crossing*, Orchard Books, New York, 1987. A thirteen-year-old Mexican boy tries to cross the border.

20. Stanek, Muriel, *We Came From Vietnam*, Albert Whitman, Morton Grove, Illinois, 1985. A photo-illustrated account of an immigrant family's experiences.

21. Whelan, G., *Goodbye Vietnam*, Random House, New York, 1992. A short novel about a Vietnamese girl who escapes as a refugee.

22. Winter, Jeanette, *Klara's New World*, Knopf, New York, 1992. A Swedish family faces many hardships when they immigrate to America in search of a better life.

8. Do You Wear Tags?

a) As I was writing *Who Belongs Here?*, I asked Thy, a former student, if I could spend an afternoon with her family. I asked her if she still had the identity tag that she wore to the United States. She showed me the tag, kept in a small white plastic bag with her family's x-rays. That is why, in *Who Belongs Here?*, Nary wears a tag around his neck on the airplane to the United States. The girl sitting on the trunk at Ellis Island also wears a tag.

b) Start with questions such as these and continue with the question matrix: Why did these children wear tags? Do you ever wear tags? Do you know people who wear tags? Are tags worn only by people?

c) Students could bring in tags and start a tag display or tag museum.

d) Students may want to make their own identity tags.

e) Students could look through books on immigrants and see how many pictures show people wearing tags. This could lead to a discussion of Ellis Island and other immigration stations. Did people who were detained on Angel Island wear tags?

9. One to Ten in Khmer and Other Languages

a) The language of the Cambodian people is Khmer. It is related to the Laotian and Thai languages. To varying degrees, some elements are common to the three languages.
Have your students try writing the numerals from one to ten in Khmer:

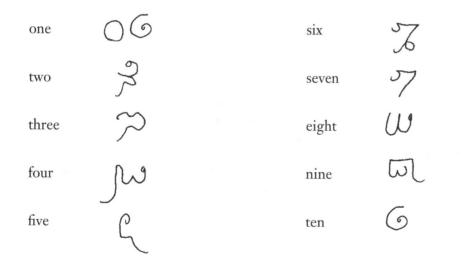

one		six	
two		seven	
three		eight	
four		nine	
five		ten	

---

b) Invite a Khmer speaker into your class to teach pronunciation of the numbers. You could do this activity with several languages and create a language wall in your classroom.

10. Hear a Word in Many Languages

a) More than three hundred languages are spoken in the United States today. How many of these languages can your students hear? Could they hear the word *friend* or learn to count to five in twenty, fifty, or one hundred languages? This would be a mighty project, but with the help of community members and parents you could gather as many languages as possible and tape them. When I work with students, there are usually at least six students who can count to five in a variety of languages.

b) Older students may want to help tape the languages and compile information about them.

c) You may want to start by having your students conduct a survey on the number of languages spoken in their classroom, school, town or city, county, state, and region. High school language students may want to help your class with this project. If you live near a college or university, use the people there as a resource.

Reading Connections

1. Haskins, Jim, *Count Your Way Through China*, Carolrhoda Books, Minneapolis, 1989. One in a series of counting books.
2. Heide, I., and J. Gilliland, *The Day of Ahmed's Secret*, Lothrop, Lee and Shepard, New York, 1990. Takes place in Cairo and introduces Arabic.
3. Levine, Ellen, *I Hate English*, Scholastic Books, New York, 1989. Story of a girl who isn't always happy to be learning English.
4. Feelings, Muriel, *A Swahili Alphabet Book*, Dial, New York, 1971.

11. Learn More About English

"Some days learning English is frustrating for Nary, but his friends and teachers are helping him. On rainy days he laughs as he tells his grandmother it's raining cats and dogs."

In any language, idiomatic expressions are by far the hardest for a newcomer to understand and learn. Idioms develop as part of the culture of a particular linguistic group. Unless one is a member of the culture or is keenly aware of the culture, idiomatic expression may sound strange and can be difficult to master.

English is a member of the Indo-European language family. It is a linguistic descendant of Sanskrit, Greek, Latin, and its offspring (French, Spanish, Italian, etc..) It is also related to the Celtic, Germanic, Baltic, and Slavic tongues. The English language borrows words and / or expressions from linguistic groups with which English speakers interact, such as users of Asian languages. The following diagram shows how modern-day English changes and develops.

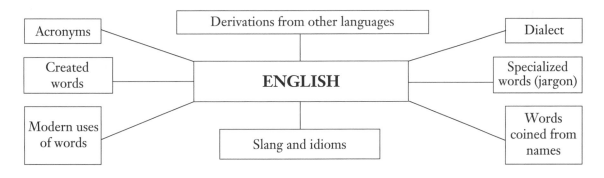

a) Idioms: Ask your students to come up with five idioms they use. Examples:

1. Chew the fat.
2. Fly by the seat of your pants.
3. Sleep like a baby.

Discuss with your class the possible origins of these idiomatic expressions. Can the students think of more idioms? Ask them to illustrate some of their idioms and display the pictures.

b) Be an Etymologist: Provide your class with copies of an etymological dictionary. Have your students try to find out what languages these words came from and their original meanings:

mountain (French, *montagne*; Spanish, *montana*)
family (French, *famille*; Spanish, *familia*)
garden (German, *garten*)
slalom (Norwegian, *slalom*)
assassin (Arabic, *hashshashin* — a band of Syrians who took hashish,
　　　an intoxicant, before engaging in massacres of Christian
　　　crusaders)
ukulele (Hawaiian, *ukulele*)
brother (German, *bruder*)
liberty (Latin, *liber*)
typhoon (Chinese, *ty fung* — big wind)
caravan (Persian, *karwan* — traveling companion)
souvenir (French, *souvenir* — to remember)

neon (Greek, *neos* — new)
academy (Greek, *Acadimie* — a garden near Athens)

c) Linguistic Sleuth Adventure: As a society changes, with new technologies, institutions, and ever-changing interpersonal relationships, so does its language. English is no exception to this rule. The following activity will help your students see how English changes and expands.

To show how names can become "household" words, give your students the list of words italicized at left and ask them to use a dictionary to discover the words' origins.

1. *watt*	James Watt (1736–1819), Scottish inventor of the steam engine.
2. *pasteurize*	Louis Pasteur (1822–1895), French scientist who invented a process used to kill bacteria in milk.
3. *silhouette*	Etienne de Silhouette (1709–1767), minister of finance of France. Known as a niggardly man, he wouldn't have full paintings, only outlines, made for his home. Many people scornfully called these black portraits *silhouettes*.
4. *vulcanize*	Vulcan, Roman god of fire.
5. *voltage*	Alessandro Volta (1745–1827), Italian physicist who discovered electricity formed by the chemical action between metals and liquids, as in a battery.
6. *iris*	Iris, Greek goddess of the rainbow, believed responsible for the brilliant colors of flowers.
7. *saxophone*	Antoine J. Sax (1814–1894), Belgian instrument maker.
8. *panic*	Pan, Greek god of nature, whose actions incited sudden fright.
9. *wellingtons*	Duke of Wellington (1769–1852); his tall military boots covered his knees.

d) Created Words: The following activity helps students gain insight into the phenomenon of how words and expressions are created to accommodate changes in society.

Encourage your students to think of some relatively new words and expressions. (The following examples will get them started.)

1. brainstorm	4. motel	7. fax
2. winterize	5. technicolor	8. paperback
3. smog	6. waterbed	9. camcorder

e) Acronyms: Many new words are actually acronyms, composed of the initial letters of other words. An example is SCUBA, which stands for Self-Contained Underwater Breathing Apparatus.

Your students will have fun finding out what the following acronyms stand for. Perhaps they can add to the list.

1. SWAT	Special Weapons And Tactics
2. MASH	Mobile Army Surgical Hospital
3. UNICEF	United Nations Children's Emergency Fund
4. SALT	Strategic Arms Limitation Talks
5. NATO	North Atlantic Treaty Organization

Reading Connections

1. Aubin, Michel, *The Secret Code*, James Lorimer, Toronto, 1987.
2. Ehlert, Lois, *Eating the Alphabet: Fruits and Vegetables From A to Z*, Harcourt Brace Jovanovich, New York, 1989.
3. Feeney, Stephanie, *A is for Aloha*, University of Hawaii, Honolulu, 1980.
4. Harrison, Ted, *A Northern Alphabet*, Tundra, Montreal, 1982.
5. Levine, Ellen, *I Hate English*, Scholastic, New York, 1989.
6. Moak, Allen, *A Big City ABC*, Tundra, Montreal, 1984.
7. Roache, Gordon, *A Halifax ABC*, Tundra, Montreal, 1987.
8. Schwartz, Alvin, *The Cat's Elbow and Other Secret Languages*, Farrar, Straus and Giroux, New York, 1982. A delightful book that stimulates language play.

12. Rice, Rice, Rice

a) "Rice, a cereal grain, is one of the world's most important foods. About one-half of the world's population lives almost entirely on a rice diet. Most of these people live in Asia, but rice is also important in the western world.

" . . . Vitamins and minerals are in the outer covering or hull. In eastern countries, it is eaten with the hull (brown rice); in western countries it is milled and the hull is removed (white rice.) Completely milled rice is called polished rice. Rice is usually cooked in water. The kernels absorb the water and double or triple their size. . . .

" . . . There are thousands of varieties of rice which vary in the height of the plants and in the length of the heads of grain. . . .

" . . . The seed is broadcast (scattered) in prepared seed beds. Later, the plants are transplanted into flat, dike-rimmed fields, called paddies. The fields are then flooded by letting in water from the canals or the river through gates in the walls which surround each field. The growers must keep at least five inches of water on the fields during the growing season.

" . . . In most countries, the harvesting is done with old fashioned sickles, for only specially made machinery can operate in the muddy fields. In a few places, the threshing and hulling are done mechanically. In Asia, rice is pounded on hollowed out logs with huge wooden mallets to clean it of its outside coating. . . .

" . . . Rice cannot be used for bread baking because it contains very little gluten (a material which holds bread dough together.) Nevertheless, it is sometimes ground into flour and made into small flat cakes or as shells for meat delicacies. . . .

" The Japanese make rice straw into hats, matting shoes and bagging. They also ferment the grain and produce a drink called sake."

Britannica Junior Encyclopaedia, Volume 13, 1982

b) Start your classroom discussion of rice with these questions:

How many of you eat rice regularly as a meal?
What kind of rice dishes do you like?
How many of you have not eaten rice?
Do you know where in the world people eat rice for breakfast, lunch, and dinner?
Where in the world is rice grown?
Is rice grown in our country? Where?
Can you think of cultural events or celebrations in which rice plays a special role?

c) On a wall world map, have students mark parts of the world where rice is produced and / or consumed with colored tacks or pins.

d) Chinese and Japanese people have long made a delicate yet absorbent watercolor art paper out of rice. Pick up some rice paper from an art supplier or Chinese specialty store. Provide children with watercolor paints and brushes. Encourage them to experiment with the paints and paper. As a followup, invite a Chinese or Japanese watercolorist to demonstrate oriental painting.

e) Food Experience — Three Rice Recipes

Simple Boiled Rice
Ingredients: 2 cups long-grain rice
4 cups water
Method:
Place rice and water in a saucepan (you may wash the rice first, if you wish, to remove any debris.) Turn the heat to high and bring to a boil. When the water boils, cover and reduce heat to simmer, cooking for another 20 minutes. Remove lid and check to see whether rice is dry and fluffy. If it isn't, turn heat to the lowest temperature and replace lid. Let rice sit for another 5 minutes. Give each child in the class a taste. You may wish to repeat the process with other rices such as brown, wild, glutinous, short-grain, basmati, etc. (Warning: the proportion of water to rice varies with the type of rice. Please check package before cooking.) Ask children to compare and contrast the different kinds of rice they have prepared.

Rice Pudding
Ingredients: 2 1/2 cups cooked rice
2 1/2 cups milk
3 tablespoons brown sugar
1 1/2 tablespoons margarine
1 cup currants or raisins

Method:

Combine everything except currants or raisins in a saucepan and cook over low heat for 20 minutes, stirring often. Add currants or raisins and continue cooking for another 10 minutes. When pudding is thickened, remove from heat and serve.

Fried Rice

Ingredients:

5 cups cold cooked rice
1/2 pound raw shelled shrimp (optional)
1/2 cup Chinese barbecued pork, or cha-siu (If this is not available, other cooked meats such as ham, salami, roast beef, etc., may be substituted.)
1/2 cup frozen mixed peas and carrots (Other firm, colorful, diced vegetables may be substituted.)
1/2 tablespoon chopped green onion
1/2 teaspoon salt
3 tablespoons soy sauce
cooking oil
2 eggs, well beaten

Method:

Sprinkle shrimp with salt. Let sit for 10 minutes. Stir-fry shrimp (turn it constantly with a spatula) at a high temperature until pink, then remove from wok or frying pan. Place 1/2 tablespoon oil in wok. Sprinkle with a pinch of salt. Pour in beaten eggs. Stir-fry at a low temperature, breaking eggs into small fragments as they cook. Remove when done.

Place 1 teaspoon of oil in wok. Add chopped green onion and stir until aromatic. Add ham or pork, stir-frying at medium heat until browned. Remove from wok.

Place peas and carrots in wok, with more oil if necessary, sprinkling with a pinch of salt. Stir-fry at high heat (to seal in moisture and flavor) until peas are a glistening green. Remove.

Heat 2 tablespoons of oil. Add rice, breaking any lumps with your clean fingers so that each grain is separate from the rest. (This is an important step, and something that young children may enjoy doing even before the stove is turned on.) Stir-fry rapidly to prevent rice from sticking to wok. Add soy sauce gradually, and in a thin stream, while stirring rice. Add all other ingredients and keep stirring constantly and rapidly for 2 minutes to combine everything. Serve while warm.

Reading Connections

1. Dooley, N., *Everybody Cooks Rice*, Carolrhoda Books, Minneapolis, 1991.
2. Sendak, M., *Chicken Soup with Rice*, Harper and Row, New York, 1962.

13. What Do You Eat Everyday?

a) Nary eats rice everyday. What do your students eat everyday?

b) After your students have brainstormed a list of the foods they eat everyday, ask them why they eat these foods. Why do they drink milk and eat bread? Why do they eat cereal and fruit?

c) Nary likes pizza and ice cream. What are your students' favorite foods? For younger students, ask them to draw or find a picture of their favorite food. Then play twenty questions until a classmate guesses the food.

d) Post a list of favorite foods, or take a class survey to discover each child's favorite food and why he / she likes it (e.g., "Susan likes carrots because she thinks they are sweet".) Each student could be responsible for interviewing a given number of children.

e) Students could poll the school staff and / or students in other classes about their favorite foods. Posters could be made to display the information.

f) Students could bring in favorite family recipes and compile a class cookbook.

g) Rice is a staple food. What are other staples, and how and why are they important? Research papers and projects could be done about major food staples in the world or regions of the United States and Canada.

h) Nary's grandmother sends money to Cambodia so relatives can buy rice seeds. Ask students if they have ever sent a letter or package to someone in another country. What is the procedure?

i) Invite to your class a community or staff member who has relatives in another country. How do they keep in touch?

14. How Many Varieties of Food?

a) Bring in several varieties of potatoes, strawberries, squash, or whatever is available. Ask your students what the foods are and how they are the same and different. Why are there different kinds of potatoes and tomatoes? You could use the question matrix to gather more information. Students may want to bring in other foods.

b) Your class may want to have a feast with one type of food. How many ways can they cook a potato or use bread?

c) Students could write menus and have a meal using foods raised in your region or other areas.

Reading Connections

1. Aliki, *Corn Is Maize: The Gift of the Indians*, A Let's Read and Find Out Science Book, Harper Collins, New York, 1976. The introduction of corn by Native Americans.

2. Machotka, Hana, *Pasta Factory*, Houghton Mifflin, Boston, 1992.
3. Meltzer, Milton, *The Amazing Potato*, Harper Collins, New York, 1992. The history of the potato.

15. Unions and United Farm Workers

a) Write to United Farm Workers (UFW), Curriculum Project, Department Pa, Box 62, Keene, CA 93531, for a free curriculum, video, and coloring book about the United Farm Workers.

b) Invite union members into your classroom.

c) Invite people who do not support unions into your classroom so students can hear opposing views.

d) *Newsies*, a Walt Disney musical, tells the story of newspaper boys in New York City who formed a union to get fair pay. It's a great introduction to unions.

Reading Connections

1. Altman, Linda Jacobs, *Amelia's Road*, Lee and Low, New York, 1993. An illustrated book about a young girl and her migrant farm worker family.
2. Atkin, S. Beth, *Voices From the Field, Children of Migrant Farmworkers Tell Their Stories*, Little, Brown, Boston, 1993.
3. de Ruiz, D., and R. Larios, *La Causa, The Migrant Farmworkers' Story*, Steck-Vaughn, New York, 1993.
4. Dorros, Arthur, *Radio Man, A Story in English and Spanish*, Harper Collins, New York, 1993. Diego and his family are migrant farm workers. As he drives with his family from state to state, he keeps his radio with him.
5. Goodwin, David, *Cesar Chavez, Hope for the People*, Fawcett Columbine, New York, 1991.
6. Morey, J., *Famous Mexican Americans*, Dutton, New York, 1989. Includes Dolores Huerta.
7. Rappaport, Doreen, *American Woman, Their Lives in Their Words*, Harper Collins, New York, 1992. Includes Dolores Huerta.

16. Build a Wall of Faces and Stories

a) Dith Pran and Dolores Huerta are two of the many people who have tried to make the world a better place. Who are some of the other people who have worked for a better world? Start locally and list all the people your students know who work for change.

b) Leave the list posted. You may want to make a list and display it next to your students' list. Locate pictures of each person.

c) Ask your students to glue the pictures on sheets of sturdy 8 x 10 paper. Each picture should be labeled with the name of the person in big, clear letters. Leave space for holes to be punched in each corner.

d) Have the students, working in groups, record what they know about each person. You may want to limit the number of names so that the groups have time to research each person.

e) Have your students find out what these people did and why. They should write down the information. You can show them what I wrote about Dith Pran and Dolores Huerta as examples. Ask them: if you had been limited to one sentence about each person, what would you have written? For Dith Pran a student may write, "Dith Pran talks about the war in Cambodia because he wants peace in his homeland." For Dolores Huerta, "For over forty years Dolores Huerta has helped farm laborers in the United States."

f) After students have written several sentences, ask them to edit their work to one sentence about the person or people they are studying. After the sentence is edited, ask them to write it neatly on the other side of the picture.

g) Once all the faces have stories, punch four holes in each paper and fasten them together with pipe cleaners six pages across. When all the papers are fastened, you'll have a "wall" that can be hung from the ceiling so that both sides show.

h) Invite the local people that your students wrote about to visit your classroom.

Reading Connections

1. Hoose, Philip, *It's Our World, Too, Stories of Young People Who Are Making a Difference*, Little, Brown, Boston, 1993.
2. Lanker, Brian, *I Dream a World, Portraits of Black Women Who Changed America*, Stewart, Tabori and Chang, New York, 1989.

17. Where Do Ideas Come From? (Constitution)

a) Writers of the United States Constitution, like the writers of other important documents, gathered ideas from different sources. Ask your students where they get their ideas and why. You could use the question matrix to expand these questions.

b) Parts of theUnited States Constitution were modeled after the Iroquois Confederacy. Why did the Iroquois form a confederation? What other agreements influenced the framers of the Constitution? Ask groups to research these questions and report to the class.

c) Identify some other important documents and find out where the people who wrote them got their ideas. Older students could research a document. With younger students, display and discuss several documents.

Reading Connections

1. Agel, Jerome, *Twelve Documents That Shaped the World*, Putnam, New York, 1992.
2. Graymont, Barbara, *The Iroquois*, Chelsea House, New York, 1988.
3. Moyers, Bill, *A World of Ideas, Public Opinions From Private Citizens*, Doubleday, New York, 1990.
4. Prolman, Marilyn, *The Story of the Constitution*, Children's Press, Chicago, 1969.
5. Weatherford, Jack, *Indian Givers, How the Indians of America Transformed the World*, Crown Publishers, New York, 1988. Chapter 8 is about the Iroquois and their link to the Constitution.

18. How Do You Feel?

a) Students could write a sentence or more about their feelings: e.g., I feel sad when _____. Afterward, ask your class to write about the feelings in *Who Belongs Here?* — either Nary's feelings or those of other characters. When they are done, they could use three different typesets or colors or printing styles to create a finished product:

> I am happy when I can ride my bike to my friend's house.
> Nary is happy when he is playing soccer.
> The Iroquois people are happy at their meeting.

b) This activity could lead to a discussion of name-calling. When I work with groups of students, I often show them the picture of Nary being teased and ask them to raise their hands if they have ever been called a name that hurt their feelings.

c) Ask each student to write down the name that would hurt them the most; then, with their permission, collect the hurtful names and make a poster. Explain to your students that their own names won't be on the poster. Display the poster and talk about the names. Why would such names hurt? What should happen when people are called names? With older students, you could continue the discussion by asking if name-calling leads to violence or hate crimes.

d) Invite a police officer or attorney into your class to talk about hate crimes.

19. The Empty Hallway

a) Read the following to your students:

"What if Nary was forced to go back to Cambodia?
"What if everyone who now lives in the United States, but whose ancestors came from another country, was forced to return to his or her homeland?

"What if everyone who lives in the United States was told to leave?

"Who would be left?"

If I had omitted the third question, who would be in the illustration? (There would be Native Americans in the hallway.) Discuss why with your students. Who were the first people in their community?

b) If your school hallway were filled with representatives of all the ethnic and racial groups that have ever lived in your community, who would be there? Students could research some of the groups.

c) Begin by making a list of questions. For example: When did these people come here and why? What did they do here? If they are no longer around, why not? What stories did they leave behind? Are new people still coming? What will your community look like in twenty-five years?

Use the walls of the school hallway to display the information in written or pictorial (perhaps a mural) form.

20. Follow Immigration Headlines

a) Today as in times past, immigration law is surrounded by controversy. In *Who Belongs Here?*, I ask who should be allowed to come to this country. If there are not enough houses, jobs, or food for the people who are already here, should we let more people come? Before you discuss this with your students, they need some understanding of the laws, who wrote them, and why. Some people feel that the United States is already overpopulated, with too few jobs to go around. Others feel that people wouldn't come if there were no jobs. Some people think that the laws have discriminated against ethnic minorities and that to be against immigration is to be racist.

b) This is a big topic and needs time to be discussed and rediscussed. If you live in an area where there are immigration officials, invite them into your class to share their views. If there are Coast Guard or Border Patrol representatives in the area, invite them to tell their stories. The Coast Guard performs many jobs related to immigration. What are they? Invite recent immigrants and people who have recent immigrants in their families. It is important to listen to all sides of the immigration issue.

c) Papers and magazines are full of immigration stories. A *USA Today* headline on July 15, 1993, said, "High Tide of Immigration Overwhelms USA." In the *Philadelphia Inquirer* on July 18, 1993, there appeared an article entitled, "Have Americans Forgotten Where They All Came From?" The *Atlantic*, October 1992, featured "Immigration and the New American Dilemma," by Jack Miles. Clarence Page, a writer for the *Chicago Tribune*, wrote an article entitled, "Making Room on the American Welcome Mat." A special fall 1993 issue of

Time magazine focused on the new face of America — how immigrants are shaping the world's first multicultural society. Attorney General Janet Reno has said, "In this decade, immigration will be the most difficult problem we face together."

d) Collect (and ask your students to collect) headlines and articles concerning immigration and post just the headlines in your classroom. Have students pick a headline and write an article without research.

e) Then ask them to read the articles that followed the headlines and talk about the information provided in each article. Where did the writer get the information? Where could you get more information? After your students have gathered more information, have them rewrite their articles.

f) Invite a media person into your classroom to talk about immigration and the media.

21. Write Your Own Immigration Laws

a) Have your students, working in groups, pretend that they are the first people of an area. Name and define that area. It could be a fictional place or one the students know.
Who were these first people, and why did they live in this area? Then tell the groups that other people want to move to their area and they need to write immigration laws. Why and how will they write these laws? What criteria will they use? Why? Their reasons must be valid, clear, and concise. When all groups are finished, post and discuss the new laws.

b) This could lead to a discussion of existing and past immigration laws. These laws could also be researched and posted. Finally, discuss future immigration laws. This may be a good time to invite an immigration official or immigration lawyer to your class. Again try to ensure that your students hear both sides of the immigration story.

22. Who Is a Real American?

The New World (North America, South America, and Australia) is inhabited by people who are indigenous to those continents and by people who immigrated there from all over the world. Some came many years ago; others are relatively new arrivals.

In the United States, Canada, Mexico, and South America, indigenous peoples can trace their ancestries through thousands of years of living in those countries. Many of them have intermarried with people from the Old World (Europe, Asia, and Africa.)

"Who is a real American (or Canadian)?" begs the question, "Are some people more American (or Canadian) than others?"

a) Pose the following questions to your class to facilitate a lively discussion.

Who is a real American / Canadian?
What do you know about the founding of America / Canada as a nation?
What does being an American / Canadian mean to you?
What does *Who Belongs Here?* say about being an American / Canadian?
What else would you like to know about being an American / Canadian?

b) Lead your class in a discussion of the American (or Canadian) experience. Ask groups of students to list some of the attractions of American and Canadian society. Each group may then design a tourism brochure aimed at describing the real Canada or United States.

c) Discuss with your class the significance of taking pride in one's ethnocultural heritage. How do people's different heritages contribute to the quality of life in America and Canada? What are some of the ways people express their culture (through the foods they eat, the language they speak, and the religion they practice)? Does the use of hyphenated terms such as Afro-American, Mexican-American, and Ukrainian-Canadian help or hinder the formation of national unity and sense of identity?

Is "melting pot" an outdated image for cultural diversity? Some people have suggested a salad bowl as a better analogy. What do your students think? Have your students draw pictures or make collages of their analogies.

Reading Connections

The following books and the ones listed under More Reading Connections on page 30 are about being or becoming an American. With the assistance of your school librarian and / or public librarian, place some books in your classroom library. Encourage your students to borrow them to supplement their reading on the theme. Help students conduct discussions sharing their reading and perceptions.

1. Sandin, Joan, *The Long Way to a New Land*, Harper Collins, New York, 1981. A Swedish family's journey to America in the 1860's.

2. Shaw, Janet, *Meet Kirsten: An American Girl*, Pleasant Company, Middleton, Wisconsin, 1986. A girl and her family learn to adjust to life on the American prairie after leaving Sweden.

23. Who Doesn't Belong Here?

a) My book asks, "What if everyone who lives in the United States was told to leave? Who would be left? Who belongs here?" Simply put, other than the indigenous peoples who have inhabited North and South America for thousands of years, all of the people who have lived on these continents either came from other parts of the world or have had ancestors who did.

"Who belongs here?" is, of course, a rhetorical question. But its corollaries, "Who doesn't belong here?" and "Who should not be here?," are real questions that have been debated again and again in legislatures, courts, the media, and classrooms.

Every nation has policies governing the admission of newcomers. Most of these policies are based upon pragmatic reasons aimed at protecting the overall welfare of citizens, although discrimination may have played a part in some immigration policies.

"Who doesn't belong here?" is an interesting topic for you and your students to explore. The question forces us to examine our unspoken fears, affinities, unchallenged beliefs, and misguided prejudices. As we examine ourselves as individuals, we can critique the policies we set collectively, as a nation.

b) "Who should be allowed to come to the United States?"

"Should anyone be made to leave?"

"If there aren't enough jobs, homes, and food for everyone, how do we decide who gets to live here?"

Lead your class in an open discussion of these questions. Record the students' statements on a large sheet of paper. Conclude with a debriefing session.

c) Give your class the address of your local immigration office. Assign them to perform a research project on policies governing refugee admission, particularly rules of exclusion (who should be kept out of the country.)

d) Lead your class in a discussion of the advantages and disadvantages of a pluralistic society, in which peoples of different cultural and linguistic backgrounds, races, ethnic groups, and religious beliefs live together.

Divide a sheet of chart paper into columns titled "Pros" and "Cons." Record your students' ideas. Ask clarifying questions, if need be, as ideas are offered. Afterward, help students draw conclusions from the discussion. Write those conclusions on another sheet of paper.

24. Giant Scrapbook — What's Your Story?

a) A K-5 school in Winthrop, Maine, launched the 1993–1994 year with a giant "What's Your Story, Winthrop, Maine?" scrapbook project. I was invited to introduce the scrapbook idea by using *Who Belongs Here?* I showed several pictures and told brief stories about Nary, but the emphasis was on the page with the scrapbook. I told the students that we all have stories to tell and to share and explained the scrapbook idea.

b) Each class designed and partially filled a large sheet of posterboard with short, one- to three-sentence stories about their names, the food they eat, their family celebrations, their heritage, and traditions they have or would like to begin. The final stories were written on fade-free colored paper.

c) Teachers sent the following letter to all parents so that they could help their children decide what to write about.

Dear Parents:

A special school-wide theme this year will be "What's Your Story?" as inspired by our local author, Margy Burns Knight. Please share any special stories with your children about your family and where you came from as far back as possible. You may have traditions you honor based on heritage, such as a certain recipes, holiday customs, etc. This is a chance to share special remembrances or knowledge about your family with all members contributing. Take time to help your child write or illustrate any family anecdotes as the year progresses. By the end of the year each student will have a collection of stories and histories about his / her family. We are looking forward to this very special project as students make connections with each other through a greater understanding of our many experiences and backgrounds. Thank you for your assistance with this project.

d) Older students started with four or five sentences and edited to one or two sentences. A kindergarten student told me he had lots of stories but hadn't learned to write yet. A fourth grader told me he had no stories. I asked him if he did anything special with his family, and he told me that his family eats donuts every Wednesday. A first grader told me her name was Polish.

e) A letter was sent to local businesses asking them to display the scrapbook pages and inviting employees to add their stories to the pages.

f) The name of the teacher and business were written in calligraphy on each page.

g) Thirty pages were displayed at local businesses for three weeks. Some classes delivered the pages to the businesses; many business people came to school to pick up the pages themselves. The local newspaper advertised where the pages would be on display.

h) After the display, the students collected, laminated, and collated the pages and bound them with large rings. A cover, endpapers, and table of contents were added. The scrapbook, containing more than one thousand stories, will be displayed again at school and throughout the community.

i) Another local school chose traditions as their theme, and each class created a traditions book.

25. On Common Ground

a) "On Common Ground, Getting It Together with Lessons From Real Life" is a *Seattle Times* reprint. The idea started with a professor's letter to the editor: couldn't the *Times* do something to help educators introduce students to people of diverse cultures and circumstances? The reprint includes a series of articles about diversity published in the *Times* from 1990 to1993. Topics include learning about other people, challenging stereotypes, what makes a family, and more. To get a copy of "On Common Ground," send $3 to the *Seattle Times*, Box 1926, Seattle, WA 98111-1926.

b) You and your students could make a similar collection of articles from local media. After they have read "On Common Ground," ask the students to find articles from local media and combine them in a booklet. They could also research and find the same types of facts and resources in your area as appear at the end of "On Common Ground."

c) Or have students write their own articles and compile them as a booklet. Students could write stories about themselves or their families or interview community members with different backgrounds.

26. Symbols of Peace

a) I wrote about peace five times in Nary's story. Nary's grandmother heard the United States was full of peace and food, and Nary wonders if there will ever be peace in Cambodia, to name two instances.

b) Ask your students to identify symbols of peace (dove, olive branch, white flag.) Why are these images peace symbols? How are they used?

c) Students could make their own peace symbols and display them with their research in the school or community library along with some of the following materials.

Aasberg, Nathan, *The Peace Seekers: Nobel Peace Prize*, Lerner, Minneapolis, 1987.

Carter, Jimmy, *Talking Peace*, Dutton, New York, 1993. Examines the causes and effects of conflict.

Coerr, Eleanor, *Sadako and the Thousand Cranes*, Putnam, New York, 1977.

Dolphin, Laurie, *Oasis of Peace*, Scholastic, New York, 1993. About a school in Israel.

Durrell, Ann, and Marilyn Sachs, eds., *The Big Book for Peace*, Dutton, New York, 1990.

Grammar, Red, *Teaching Peace*, Smiling Atcha Music, Peekskill, New York, 1980. Audiocassette.

Knight, Margy Burns, *Talking Walls*, Tilbury House, Gardiner, Maine, 1992.

Maruki, Toshi, *Hiroshima No Pika*, Lothrop, Lee and Shepard, New York, 1990.

Scholes, Katherine, *Peace Begins with You*, Little, Brown, Boston, 1990.

Seuss, Dr., *The Butter Battle Book*, Random House, New York, 1984.

27. What Is Fair?

Children innately recognize what is fair and what is not. However, like most people, when they are under pressure, they may overlook fairness and twist situations to their advantage. This unit aims at helping children understand fairness on a conscious level, so that they may exercise fairness in their daily lives.

Related to the notion of fairness are three other concepts that deserve clarification: freedom, equality, and human rights. Inherent in a democratic system of government, such as the governments of the United States, Canada, and western Europe, is a belief in the freedom of individuals to live productive lives (please refer to Teacher's Notes.)

It is appropriate to teach children that individual freedoms should be exercised and enjoyed insofar as the legitimate freedoms of others are not violated or suppressed as a result. As stated in Article 29 of the United Nations' Universal Declaration of Human Rights, individuals are entitled to exercise their rights and freedoms only to the extent that they do not infringe unreasonably on the rights and freedoms of others. Similarly, we can point out to children that they may do and say what they like as long as they do not hurt others in the process. For example, most people would agree that individuals do not have a right to call other people names when people are hurt as a result. Consider how Nary felt when other students called him a "chink."

Children should also learn that fairness does not necessarily mean equality. Fairness connotes relativity. It is meaningful only within the context of a situation. For example, children who have completed their classwork may enjoy "choice time" for reading or writing, whereas those who have not done so must complete their assignments during choice time. That's fairness. In the adult world, it is considered fair that income tax is levied relative to one's income.

Equality, on the other hand, does not take into account individual differences but applies to everyone in all situations. For example, the Universal Declaration of Human Rights asserts that "all human beings are born free and equal in dignity and rights." A practical application of the concept of equality appears in equal employment opportunities for men and women, the able-bodied, the physically handicapped, and people of all ethnocultural backgrounds.

In the classroom, equality may mean that all children have an equal opportunity to enjoy the privilege of choice time so long as their assignments are completed satisfactorily. However, if children expect absolute equality, regardless of their efforts, they misunderstand the principle of equality. We should discuss with children whether equality is fair in a given instance. Justice is achieved only when fair treatment and equal opportunity coexist (please refer to Teacher's Notes.)

The following suggested activities aim at helping children become more sensitive to interacting fairly with one another through conscious decision-making while taking into account individual rights, freedom, and equality.

a) Write on the chalkboard the following headings: Fairness, Freedom, Rights, and Equality. Divide your class into groups of three. Each group receives a felt pen and a sheet of chart paper with one of the four headings on it. Give each group clear directions in: (a) designating a recorder who will write the group's ideas on the chart paper; (b) brainstorming (from their personal experiences) at least three situations in which one of the four ideals was applicable; (c) collectively coming up with a workable definition of the term given; (d) posting at the front of the classroom the information the recorders have written and presenting to the class what they have discussed and agreed upon as definitions.

Under your guidance, your class should have enough material for a lively discussion about fairness, freedom, rights, and equality. You may choose to debrief at the end of the discussion.

b) As a followup, devote a lesson to discussing how we exercise fairness in the classroom, on the school grounds, at home, and with friends.

Write down your students' ideas on a sheet of chart paper. From the ideas collected, you may guide your class to draft a Classroom Code of Ethics (or Code of Behavior, depending on the age of your children), in which every child has ownership. As a class, you may decide on methods of reinforcement with appropriate logical and natural consequences.

c) For older students, provide an opportunity to research and write about several examples of social injustice in our society. The students should suggest solutions to the problems they describe.

d) Divide your class into groups of three. Give each group one of the following scenarios to role-play. After role-playing, provide ample opportunity for your students to discuss the activity and the emotions it evoked.

Scenario 1: You are a conscientious student who seldom leaves work uncompleted. This morning, in your hurry to get to school, you left your social studies project on the kitchen table. Your social studies instructor is a fair but no-nonsense teacher. The consequences for a late assignment are a deduction of ten points and a detention, and he applies that consequence equally to all who fail to comply with his rules.

Hoping that the teacher would overlook an accidental slip-up, you had gone to see him before class. To your disappointment, he refused. He insisted that the consequence for lateness is applied universally, fairly, and without exceptions. How do you feel? What are you going to do about the situation and your feelings?

Scenario 2: Your parents ground you after a complaint by your school principal. You fought with a schoolmate, and when a teacher intervened, you swore at the teacher in a moment of anger.

Your cousins come for a visit. As punishment for your offense at school, you are not allowed to accompany your cousins on a tour around town. Instead, your sister and brother will be the tour hosts. You feel that the consequence is pretty unfair. What are you going to do about it?

Scenario 3: Your class was assigned a research project a month ago. You had the option of doing the project by yourself or doing it with a partner. You and Johnny were keen on doing it together.

As soon as the assignment was given, you and Johnny planned and organized your respective tasks. You went right to work on your half of the project and were proud of what you accomplished. But when you and Johnny met one week before the deadline, you discovered that Johnny had done very little. Now you are upset. What should you do?

e) A Discussion: Is name-calling fair? How would you feel if someone called you a name? How do you think Nary felt? How do we deal with victimizing behavior in school?

f) Provide an opportunity for each student to conduct an opening exercise / activity at the beginning of the school day (be it leading the national anthem, reading an inspirational passage, and / or arranging the weather chart and calendar for the day.) Allow the student to command the attention of his / her classmates in any way they see fit.

After every student has had an opportunity to lead, devote a lesson to exploring their feelings about having or not having control in conducting the opening exercise.

Encourage your students to express their feelings. Guide them to empathize with others who, because of name-calling or other kinds of victimization, have lost a feeling of control over their lives.

g) Puppet shows are particularly effective with younger children (kindergarten to third grade.) Pose four different scenarios involving unfair behaviors (perhaps one on bullying, one on name-calling, one on theft, and another on lying or bearing false witness to another child) and thoroughly discuss with your class the sequence of events, hurt feelings and / or other injuries caused, what caused the unfair behavior, and how the conflict may be resolved.

Construct a puppet stage out of a large cardboard appliance box. Remove one side of the box. Create a stage window approximately 2.5 feet x 1.5 feet by cutting with a sharp blade. Fold the resulting flap down at the bottom of the window as a stage platform. Trim the platform to six inches wide by folding the flap and then taping the flap to the body of the box, thus creating a support for the platform. Refer to the diagram on the following page.

You can make puppets out of socks with faces drawn or taped on them. Or they can be made out of construction paper attached to popsicle sticks, chopsticks, or dowels.

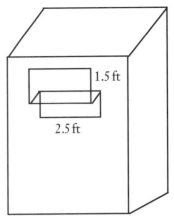

1.5 ft

2.5 ft

h) For each theme / topic you are teaching, you may want to provide your students with related books, posters, photographs, and other materials. One fun way to ensure equal access to these materials is to place them in a cloth bag, either purchased or homemade, about the size of a standard grocery bag. Students take turns signing out the theme bag and taking it home for several days. Parents receive a note explaining the purpose of the bag and are encouraged to take part in the activities with their children, such as reading the books to them and discussing the theme.

Reading Connections

1. Ball, John, *In the Heat of the Night*, Perennial, New York, 1985.
2. Estes, Eleanor, *The Hundred Dresses*, Harcourt Brace Jovanovich, New York, 1974. A girl faces a crisis of conscience when the victim of her teasing moves away. It is too late for her to make amends.
3. Everett, Louise, *Amigo Means Friends*, Troll Associates, Mahwah, N.J., 1988. Friends can be people from different cultural and linguistic backgrounds.
4. Fisher, Leonard Everett, *A Russian Farewell*, Four Winds Press, New York, 1980. Due to anti-Semitic sentiment in Russia, a Jewish family decides to say farewell to their homeland.
5. Keats, Ezra Jack, *Goggles!*, Macmillan, New York, 1969. A story of two boys who outwit neighborhood bullies.
6. Mills, Lauren, *The Rag Coat*, Little, Brown, Boston, 1991. A girl wins the friendship of those who once teased her by showing them forgiveness and love.
7. Wallace, Ian, and Angela Wood, *The Sandwich*, Kids Can Press, University of Toronto Press, Toronto, 1975. The strong smell of a boy's favorite sandwich meat and cheese repels his friends — until they taste the sandwich.
8. Wilson, Beth P., *Jenny*, Macmillan, New York, 1990. One girl's dreams and prayers for peace, love, and harmony.

28. Play a New Game

a) As I wrote *Who Belongs Here?*, I tried to balance the grim side of Nary's story with the joy in his life. He plays soccer and the drums and enjoys joking with his grandmother. I didn't mention a lot of the fun my Cambodian students have shown us — the kites they make, their love of chess, the traditional Cambodian games they taught us.

b) Have your students write about their favorite games and read books about games.

c) Find someone in your community who knows "new games" and is willing to teach one to your students. Then your class can teach it to another class.

Reading Connections

1. Lankford, Mary D., *Hopscotch Around the World*, Morrow Junior Books, New York, 1992.
2. Martel, Cruz, *Yagua Days*, Scholastic, New York, 1976. About a game in Puerto Rico.
3. Park, M., and S. Panik, *A Quetzalcoatl Tale of the Ball Game*, Simon and Schuster, New York, 1992.
4. Yolen, Jane, ed., *Street Rhymes From Around the World*, Boyd Mill Press, Pennsylvania, 1992.

29. I Belong Here: An Immigrant Story

My name is Tom Chan, or Thomas Vincent Chan when I want to be formal, or simply Tom to my friends. I was born as Chan Kin Kwok, my Chinese name given lovingly and proudly by my parents. "Kin Kwok" literally means "Builder of a Nation" — such was my parents' high aspiration for me! Chan is my family name, and in China, the family name comes before the given names. This confuses many non-Chinese.

I was born in the British Crown Colony of Hong Kong, a city situated at the southeastern end of the continent of Asia. Mine was an extended family, with my parents, my paternal grandmother, and three younger brothers in the same household. Polygamy was a status symbol, and since my grandfather was a successful merchant in Canton, he had four wives. As a result, I had four paternal grandmothers and twenty-three uncles and aunts, all of whom lived in a single city block of row housing. I lived within a network of kinfolk. We used to visit each other back and forth. On birthdays and festive occasions (which were many), the entire family of more than thirty people held celebratory dinners in our roof-garden. Aunts, uncles, and grandmothers were my babysitters when my parents went out.

My father worked for the British government in the Colony's Treasury Department. He was well-schooled in the classics of both China and Britain, and so was my mother, a nurse and schoolteacher. Believing that the best investment they could make for their children was a sound education, my parents sent me to a top-notch British parochial school.

The culture in which I grew up was certainly unique. At home, traditional Chinese culture and language were practiced. But I was equally at ease with the many other cultures represented in Hong Kong — British, continental European, American, Indian, Pakistani, and Philipino, to name a few. I became acutely aware of the prevailing social strata and the prejudices that kept the system alive. To put it simply, Caucasians were at the top of the social ladder, then came the Chinese, and other racial groups took up various lower positions in Hong Kong society. No one questioned those prejudices and the inequities that went with them. It was many years later that I realized that this is a chief characteristic of a colonial political system.

My parents had wanted me to pursue a university education overseas for the simple reason that I might broaden my cultural horizon. I am, to this day, indebted to them for their vision. A Canadian university was selected because Canada is part of the British Commonwealth. My parents had already thought of the academic edge I would hold were I to return to Hong Kong to pursue my career. I enrolled in a program leading toward a liberal arts degree at the University of Manitoba in the prairie city of Winnipeg, in the center of Canada.

Arriving in a strange country where the language and customs are so markedly different was quite an experience for a young man of twenty. I arrived at Winnipeg International Airport with three large suitcases that were to be my closet and drawers for some time to come. The question of where I was to stay that night never occurred to me. My overriding thought was to get to the university campus from the airport. After all, that was why I had come to Canada in the first place, I thought. If not for the Chinese Christian Fellowship of the University of Manitoba, which had set up a reception booth at the airport welcoming wide-eyed and confused newcomers like me, I would have ended up camping on the front lawn of the university Administration Building for the night! I was billeted with a family, with whom I stayed for several months until I found lodging on campus.

Understanding most of what I heard in English was not too hard for me. However, it took me several years to shed my extremely formal English and adopt the more casual style of conversational English. Like Nary in *Who Belongs Here?*, I had great difficulty with Canadian idioms. Speaking, reading, and writing the Queen's English was one thing, but understanding a phrase such as "Where's the beef?" was quite something else! This might explain my interest in English etymology and sociolinguistics.

My first degree led to other fields of study, such as law and anthropology. I eventually entered the Faculty of Education, where I earned my certification to teach. After a very positive student-teaching experience in a junior high school, I was convinced that I had found my calling. Coincidentally, my first teaching assignment was at that same junior high school, teaching language arts. I eventually earned a master's degree in education.

In my early teaching career, I was awarded a Canadian Federation of Teachers award for an audiovisual approach to teaching poetry. After a brief experience with teaching high school English, I became involved with curriculum design.

A year's sabbatical leave gave me an opportunity to complete my M.Ed., after which I accepted an invitation to teach elementary school. Those were also rewarding years. I learned what good teaching was all about. I discovered the joy of facilitating learning through a variety of instructional approaches and techniques. I was lucky to receive two prestigious teaching awards in my last year of teaching before becoming a school administrator. Although I now play a different role in the educational system, I remain keenly interested in teaching and learning. I contribute my ideas through professional journals and books and deliver professional development seminars for educators.

Meanwhile, my wife Debbie and I enjoy our four boys, ranging in age from 7 to 13. Our home is a multicultural microsociety. Debbie is of Norwegian-British-German extraction and our children have both Norwegian and Chinese names! Our 13-year-old's first name is Mons, after his maternal grandfather. His Chinese name is Tien-Yun, which means "Benevolence of Heaven." Our 11-year-old's name is Erik, and his Chinese name is Tien-Yee, meaning "Justice of Heaven." Our 9-year-old is Mikael. His Chinese name is Tien Doe, which means "The Way of Heaven." And, our youngest son, Konrad, is Tien-Duc, "Virtues of Heaven." The boys' Chinese names are the four dominant virtues of the classical Chinese culture propounded by the famous Chinese sage and scholar Confucius in the sixth and fifth centuries, B.C.

I have lived a quarter of a century in this great country, Canada, my beloved adopted home. In Canada, we enjoy a social policy of multiculturalism. Our Parliament has passed laws enforcing that policy, and the Canadian Constitution enshrines its worth. It would be naive to assume that racial conflict and discrimination do not exist in Canada. As in most things, there is a discrepancy between theory and reality. I have experienced first-hand disturbing incidents of racial prejudice, such as the time when a woman strongly objected to a Chinese person teaching her granddaughter English, and the time when a group of mis-guided junior high students taunted me with racial slurs in the school where I taught. How-ever, those experiences have been few and far between. As an educator, I have an opportunity to help children appreciate the gift of multiculturalism. I work hard to develop and implement educational programs that promote multiculturalism and combat racism.

I believe in the power of positive vision and action, which I call "the power of the rain-bow." One day, the people of the world will live in pluralistic harmony. As a former immi-grant to the New World, I never doubt where I belong. I belong here.

a) Autobiographies: This chapter is a condensed version of an autobiography. Invite your students to write their own autobiographical accounts and share them with the class.

Encourage your students to write to Tom Chan concerning his immigrant experience. His mailing address is: 146 Campbell Street, Winnipeg, Manitoba, Canada R3N 1B2.

b) Current Affairs: Ask students to follow media coverage related to the transition of Hong Kong from British to Chinese rule in 1997.

More Reading Connections

1. Anderson, Margaret, *The Journey of Shadow Bairns*, Knopf, New York, 1980. A young Scottish girl moves to Canada.

2. Bartone, Elisa, *Peppe the Lamplighter*, Lothrop, Lee and Shepard, New York, 1993. By working as a lamplighter on the streets of New York, a young Italian immigrant helps to support his family.

3. Bode, Janet, *New Kids in Town: Oral Histories of Immigrant Teens*, Scholastic, New York, 1989. Eleven teenagers from various countries give vivid accounts of leaving their homelands and adjusting to life in America.

4. Garza, Carmen Lomas, *Family Pictures: Cuardo de Familia, Story and Pictures*, Children's Book Press, San Francisco, 1990. The author's bilingual account of her childhood experiences.

5. Castile, Rand, *The Way of Tea*, Weathe, New York, 1971. The ceremony of serving tea by the Japanese is explored for its relationship to art, aesthetics, philosophy, and social custom.

6. Clapp, Patricia, *Constance*, Morrow, New York, 1968. The story, in journal format, of the arrival of a family in America on the *Mayflower* in 1620.

7. Coerr, Eleanor, *Chang's Paper Pony*, Harper Collins, New York, 1988. A Chinese immigrant boy realizes his wish of having a pony.

8. Conlon-McKenna, Marita, *The Wildflower Girl*, Holiday, New York, 1992. A teenager leaves Ireland in 1850 to come to Boston for a new life.

9. Dorris, Michael, *Morning Girl*, Hyperion, New York, 1992.

10. Flourney, Valerie, *The Patchwork Quilt*, Dial, New York, 1985. By finishing a patchwork quilt begun by her grandmother, Tanya unites her family's past and present.

11. Galicich, Anne, *The German Americans*, Chelsea House, New York, 1989. One in a series of immigration books.

12. Girard, Linda, *Walvoor, We Adopted You, Benjamin Koo*, Albert Whitman, Morton Grove, Illi-nois, 1989. A 9-year-old Korean boy is adopted by American parents.

13. Hamilton, Virginia, *Many Thousand Gone: African Americans From Slavery to Freedom*, Knopf, New York, 1993. Stories of the forced journeys of men and women from Africa to the New World.

14. Hammon, Trudy, *Haiti*, Franklin Watts, New York, 1988.

15. Hewett, Joan, *Hector Lives in the United States Now*, Harper Collins, New York, 1990. The illustrated story of a Mexican-American child.

16. Jenness, Aylette, *Come Home with Me, A Multi-Cultural Treasure Hunt*, New Press, New York, 1993.

17. Kroll, Stephen, *Mary McLean and St. Patrick's Day Parade*, Scholastic, New York, 1991.

18. Lee, Marie G., *Finding My Voice*, Houghton Mifflin, Boston, 1992. About a Korean-American girl's senior year in high school.

19. Leighton, Maxinne Rhea, *An Ellis Island Christmas*, Viking, New York, 1992. A Polish girl spends her Christmas on Ellis Island with her mother and brother while awaiting admission into America and eventually enjoys a reunion with her father.

20. Levine, Ellen, *If Your Name Was Changed at Ellis Island*, Scholastic, New York, 1992. Information about immigration through questions, answers, and pictures.

21. Littlechild, George, *This Land Is My Land*, Children's Book Press, San Francisco, 1993. What it's like to be a modern Native American artist.

22. Lyons, Mary E., *Letters From a Slave Girl*, Scribner's, New York, 1992.

23. Morey, J. A., *Famous Asian Americans*, Dutton, New York, 1992. Includes Haing Noir, the actor who played Dith Pran in *The Killing Fields*.

24. Pack, Min, *Aekyung's Dream*, Children's Book Press, San Francisco, 1988. A Korean girl struggles to adjust to life in America.

25. Say, Allen, *Grandfather's Journey*, Houghton Mifflin, Boston, 1993. A Japanese immigrant falls in love with America but retains nostalgia for his homeland.

26. Shefelman, Janice, *A Peddler's Dream*, Houghton Mifflin, Boston, 1992. A Lebanese man who moves to America realizes a dream after several setbacks.

27. Shiefman, Vicki, *Good-bye to the Trees*, Atheneum, New York, 1993. Lonely and apprehensive, a Russian teenager immigrates to Massachusetts to start a new life.

28. Sterling, D., *Tear Down the Walls, History of the American Civil Rights Movement*, Doubleday, New York, 1968.

29. Tran, Kim-Lan, *Tet: The New Year*, Simon and Schuster, New York, 1992. From a series that also includes books on Carnival, Fiesta, and Kwanzaa.

30. Wheeler, M. J., *First Came the Indians*, Macmillan Children's Group, New York, 1983. Introduces diverse Native American cultures.

31. Wolfman, Ira, *Do People Grow on Family Trees?, Geneaology for Kids and Other Beginners, The Official Ellis Island Handbook*, Workman Publishing, New York, 1991.

30. Musical Anthology for *Who Belongs Here?*

Here is a list of songs chosen by composer Justine Denison to accompany each illustration in *Who Belongs Here?* These songs were collected from some of today's best performing artists. Anthologies including many of these works can be found in the Music for Little People catalog, P.O. Box 1460, Redway, CA 95560. Many of the songs can also be found in *Rise Up Singing: The Group Singing Songbook*, a valuable collection of words, chords, and sources to 1,200 songs published by Sing Out Publications, P.O. Box 5253, Bethlehem, PA 18015-0253, or call 215-865-5366.

Illustration	Song	Composer
Cover	Turning of the World	Ruth Pelham
Inside cover	A Place in the Choir	Bill Staines
Family	Family Tree	Tom Chapin
Nary's drawing	Kid's Peace Song	Peter Alsop
Night walk	1492	Nancy Schimmel
Ellis Island	Woyaya	T. Ose, L. Amao, S. Amarfia, R. Bedau, W. Richardson, R. M. Bailey, and M. Tontoh
Ellis Island	Two Worlds	Roger Miller from *Big River*
Signs (languages)	Hello	Linda Arnold
Shopping (food)	I Am a Pizza	Peter Alsop
	Banana	Flor de Cana
Farm laborers	Pastures of Plenty	Woody Guthrie
	What Can One Little Person Do?	Sally Rogers
Six Nations Convention	Voices	Holly Near
Nary	Don't Play with Bruno	Tom Chapin
Empty hallway	Who Belongs Here?	Justine Denison
Moonlight boat	Somos El Barco	Lorre Wyatt
No Irish	Listen Mr. Bigot	Adrienne and Bob Clairborne
Freedom march	We Shall Overcome	Z. Horton, F. Hamilton, G. Carawan, and Pete Seeger
Role playing	What Do I Do?	Ruth Pelham
	Wonderful World	L. Singer and Hy Zaret
Scrapbook	The Grandma Song	Ruth Pelham
Class yearbook	Love Grows One By One	Carol Johnson
	Mir / Peace	Lorre Wyatt
	Calypso Freedom	B. Johnson Reagon and E. M. Harris
	Don't Ever Take Away My Freedom	Peter Yarrow
Cover	From a Distance	Julie Gold
	Same Boat Now	Betsy Rose

Teacher's Notes

Human Rights in the School, a guidebook published by the Manitoba Human Rights Commission, succinctly distinguishes between fairness and equality:

"Systemic discrimination results where a general practice which is applied to all similarly, is in fact a disadvantage to a particular group. An example is a hiring policy which specifies that applicants must be over 5' 11" (or 1.7 meters) tall. Such a policy would disproportionately exclude female and Asian applicants, the majority of whom are shorter than 5' 11". Favoured by this policy are Caucasian men, a substantial proportion of whom are taller than 5' 11". (Such discrimination may be justified, however, if being 5' 11" in height is proven to be a reasonable requirement for the job and is imposed in good faith.)

"In order to ensure that everyone is being treated equally, we must re-examine not only our intentions and our policies and practices but the results of a given system. . . .

"Equality does not necessarily mean treating everyone the same. True equality is achieved when everyone has equal access to the benefits that society has to offer. This may require different treatment in order to accommodate the special needs of individuals and groups. For example, ensuring that a student who is learning disabled receives an education comparable to that of non-disabled peers may require that the school or school division not only integrate the student into a 'regular' classroom, but also provide additional resources for that student."

— Manitoba Human Rights Commission, 1991

The Universal Declaration of Human Rights

In 1948, the United Nations drafted and passed the Universal Declaration of Human Rights as "a common standard of achievement for all peoples and all nations. . . ." The document contains thirty articles, the first of which affirms that "All human beings are born free and equal in dignity and rights." The Declaration also asserts each person's right to life, liberty, security, equality, democracy, justice, and basic social and economic rights.

The Constitution of the United States

The first ten amendments to the Constitution, collectively called the Bill of Rights, were proposed by Congress in 1789, and ratification was completed in 1791. The numbered amendments deal with (1) freedom of religion, speech, press, assembly, and petition, (2) the right to keep and bear arms, (3) quartering of soldiers, (4) security from unreasonable search and seizure, (5) general rights of the accused and due process of law, (6) rights of the accused before and during trial, (7) right to trial by jury in civil cases, (8) prohibitions against excessive bail and fines and against cruel and unusual punishment, (9) reservation of unenumerated rights to the people, and (10) reservation of unenumerated powers to the states or the people.

Canadian Charter of Rights and Freedoms

Part 1 of Canada's Constitution Act (1982) is entitled "Canadian Charter of Rights and Freedoms." The Charter, like the Universal Declaration of Human Rights and the American Bill of Rights, guarantees fundamental and inalienable rights for every Canadian. It guarantees fundamental freedoms of (a) conscience and religion, (b) thought, belief, opinion, and expression, including freedom of the press and other media, (c) peaceful assembly, and (d) association.

The Charter also guarantees every Canadian citizen's democratic rights; mobility; and rights pertaining to equality, official language, minority language education, and the law.

Declaration of the Rights of the Child (UNICEF, 1959)

1. All children have the right to what follows, no matter what their race, colour, sex, language, religion, political or other opinion, or where they were born or who they were born to.

2. You have the special right to grow up in a healthy and normal way, free and with dignity.

3. You have a right to a name and to be a member of a country.

4. You have the right to good food, housing and medical care.

5. You have the right to special care if handicapped in any way.

6. You have the right to love and understanding, preferably from parents, but from the government when you have no parent.

7. You have the right to go to school for free, to play, and to have an equal chance to be what you are and to learn to be responsible and useful.

8. You have the right always to be among the first to get help.

9. You have the right not to be harmed and not to be hired for work until old enough.

References for Teachers and Parents

1. Allen, Judy, *Cultural Awareness for Young Children*, Addison-Wesley, New York, 1992. Includes many cultural activities and extensive bibliographies.

2. American Friends Service Committee, 1501 Cherry Street, Philadelphia, PA 19102. Distributes *The Wabanakis of Maine and the Maritimes*, a resource book about the Penobscot, Passamaquoddy, Maliseet, Micmac, and Abenaki Indians. Also has information on native and border issues.

3. Campaign to Oppose the Return of the Khmer Rouge, 318 4th Street, N.E., Washington, DC 20002 (202-544-8446.) A coalition of forty-six humanitarian relief, public policy, and peace organizations.

4. Cohn, Amy, ed., *From Sea to Shining Sea: A Treasury of American Folklore and Folk Songs*, Scholastic, New York, 1993. A rich resource for stories and art from Native American creation myths to tales of Paul Bunyan and stories brought by recent immigrants.

5. Derman-Sparks, Louise, *Anti-Bias Curriculum, Tools for Empowering Young Children*, National Association for the Education of Young Children, Washington, D.C., 1989.

6. Drew, Naomi, *Learning the Skills of Peacemaking*, Jalmar Press, Rolling Hills Estates, California, 1987.

7. Educators for Social Responsibilty, 23 Garden Street, Cambridge, MA 02138. Call 1-800-370-2515 to order "Resources for Empowering Young Children."

8. Grabin, Monica, *Singing History*, 137 Sea Road, Kennebunk, ME 04043. A series of programs blending the music and history of the United States. Audiocassette, $10.

9. Heritage Key Catalogue, 6102 E. Mescal, Scottsdale, AZ 85254 (602-483-3313; Fax, 602-483-9666.) Lists new books.

10. Parenting for Peace and Justice Network, 4144 Lindell Boulevard, 3124 St. Louis, MO 63108. Publishes a newsletter and curriculum guides.

11. Pauly, Vivian, *You Can't Say You Can't Play*, Harvard Press, Cambridge, Massachusetts, 1992. Account of a kindergarten teacher who starts a "you-can't-say-you-can't-play" policy in her classroom.

12. *Responsive Classroom*, Northeast Foundation for Children, Greenfield, Massachusetts, 1992. A guide to teaching children to care about each other.

13. *Rethinking Schools*, 1001 E. Keefe Avenue, Milwaukee, WI 53212 (414-964-9646.) A quarterly journal for teachers, $10/yr.

14. Rogers, Vicki, *All the Colours of the Rainbow: A Teacher's Guide*, Pacific Educational Press, University of British Columbia, Vancouver, B.C., 1990.

15. Rogers, Vicki, *Apple's Not the Only Pie: A Multicultural Storybook*, Pacific Educational Press, University of British Columbia, Vancouver, B.C., 1990.

16. Rogers, Vicki, *Apple's Not the Only Pie: A Teacher's Guide*, Pacific Educational Press, University of British Columbia, Vancouver, B.C., 1990.

17. Smith, Jeff, *The Frugal Gourmet and Our Immigrant Ancestors*, Avon, New York, 1992. Recipes for your cooking projects.

18. Takaki, Ron, *A Different Mirror: A History of Multicultural America*, Little, Brown, Boston, 1993.

19. Takaki, Ron, *From Different Shores*, Oxford University Press, New York, 1987. Perspectives on race and ethnicity in America.

20. Southern Poverty Law Center, 400 Washington Avenue, Montgomery, AL 36104. Publishes the magazine *Teaching Tolerance*, a must for every classroom.

21. West Music Company, 208 Fifth Street, P.O. Box 5521, Coralville, IA 52241 (1-800-397-9378.) Catalogue lists books, recordings, videos, and choral music from many cultures including traditional music of Cambodia.

22. "What To Tell Your Child About Prejudice and Discrimination," National Parent-Teacher Association and the Anti-Defamation League of B'nai B'rith. Write to National PTA, 700 North Rush Street, Chicago, IL 60611-2571 (312-787-0977.)

23. Wiederhold, Chuck, *The Question Matrix, Cooperative Learning and Critical Thinking*, Resources for Teachers, Inc., 27128 B Paseo Espada #622, San Juan Capistrano, CA 92675 (1-800-Wee-Coop.) The question matrix that we describe in this guide comes from this book.

24. *Refugees*, United Nations High Commissioner for Refugees. A magazine distributed free of charge. Write to UNHCR in Canada (Suite 401, 280 Albert Street, Ottawa, Ontario) or in the United States (1718 Connecticut Avenue, N.W., Suite 200, Washington, D.C. 20009.)

25. Zinn, Howard, *A People's History of the United States*, Harper and Row, New York, 1980.

26. Zinn, Howard, *The Twentieth Century, A People's History*, Harper and Row, New York, 1980.

Tilbury House, Publishers

2 Mechanic Street
Gardiner, Maine 04345

Text designed on Crummett Mountain by Edith Allard, Somerville, Maine
Editing and production by Mark Melnicove, Lisa Reece, and Devon Phillips
Printing and binding by InterCity Press, Rockland, Massachusetts